The Power to Advance

*A Devotional Study to
Experience the Power of God
and the God of Power*

By Bruce H. Clark

Copyright © 2004 by Bruce H. Clark

The Power to Advance
by Bruce H. Clark

Printed in the United States of America

ISBN 1-594676-34-8

All rights reserved solely by the author. The author guarantees all contents are original and do not infringe upon the legal rights of any other person or work. No part of this book may be reproduced in any form without the permission of the author. The views expressed in this book are not necessarily those of the publisher.

Unless otherwise indicated, Bible quotations are taken from the King James Version. Copyright © 1964 by B. B. Kirkbride Bible Company.

www.xulonpress.com

I dedicate this book to the legacy of my father, the late Henry Mack Clark, Jr., a servant of God. Let the legacy grow.

Introduction

The Power to Advance is designed to assist you in moving closer to God. Over the next 40 days, these devotionals will help you become more aware of your need for God and grow in your relationship with Him on a daily basis.

Why 40 days?

There appears to be something special about the number 40 in the Bible. Jesus fasted 40 days before launching His ministry. Israel wandered 40 years in the desert before entering the "Promised Land." *The Power to Advance* will help you as a serious seeker of God, walk with Him for 40 days and gain strength to continue in Him.

Many of the devotionals are the direct result of my father's influence in my life. On April 4, 2002 my dad died, but he left such a wonderful spiritual legacy for me. His constant reminder to trust God has helped me understand that intimacy with God is the core of life. As you will see, this is a prevalent theme throughout the book.

Finally, you will also observe many of my life experiences in *The Power to Advance*. This is largely due to my father's influence as well. Dad demonstrated by word and example that faith ought to be manifested in life.

The Power to Advance's aim is to help you see how your relationship with God can be integrated into your daily life. As such, my prayer is that you will advance daily. Go beyond your current level of relationship with God and experience Him in new ways. Experience God in your family. Experience God in your work. Experience God in your play. Life is found as you experience God. This is the only way to truly ADVANCE.

Bruce Clark

Touch Him

"Somebody touched me." – Luke 8:46

Remember the story...the streets are crowded. I picture it as a cloudy, humid day. There is a multitude of people seeking to gain something from Jesus. Some have great expectation towards the possibility of meeting the Lord. Others are severely frustrated because too many people are getting to Jesus before them. Yet, even more people stand back and observe with doubt and speculation. As the Lord moves gracefully through the crowd, there is much conversation, competition, and confusion. Many people are attempting to grab Jesus and His twelve police-like disciples are there to guard off those who might be too unruly. Jesus moves along and then suddenly His spiritual reservoir is less full.

He stops in the middle of the crowd with the facial expression of a mother who has heard the voice of her lost child within a mass of people. Upon observing Jesus, the crowd also stops. They gasp, "Ahhhh." Something is going on with Jesus. Then Jesus utters the words of the completely obvious reality, "Somebody touched me."

God is looking for those who will stand out in the crowd with demonstrated faith that touches Him. Like the woman in the story, your faith can touch God. You will face obstacles and crowds of people and things may be in your way. But you can distinguish yourself in the eyes of God today by your persistent drive to reach Him. When you do this, God will meet your every need.

Do what it takes to get to God. Touch Him!

POWER QUESTION
What will you do today that will touch the heart of God?

POWER THOUGHT
I distinguish myself in the eyes of God by my persistent drive to reach Him.

POWER PRAYER
Father, I need you every hour. I need your touch, your love and your mercy. I receive your love right now. To you, I give all of the praise and honor. Oh, how I desire to see you, to touch you, to be with you. As the deer pants for the water, so my soul longs for you. You are what I'm after. It's all about you. It's all about you.

Touch Him Again

"Somebody touched me." – Luke 8:46

In the midst of the crowd there is a little lady. I imagine her to be about 5 feet and 100 lbs. At some point the night before she says with great expectation, "Tomorrow is my day! Tomorrow is the day that I meet the Lord and He solves my problem." And what a problem she had! For twelve years, she has had a continuous menstrual cycle. She is stigmatized by all of the women in town because of it. For twelve long, painful, shameful years, Doctors can only say, "I'm sorry." She wakes up on the morning of our story, like an underdog sure of victory, but aware of the challenges ahead. She says in her heart, "Regardless of how many people are there today, no matter how far Jesus is away from me, I will touch the Lord." She gets to the streets only to realize that there are too many people to count; far more than she had in mind.

The little lady thinks, "I may not be able to see all of Jesus. I may not press all the way to him. But, if I can touch the hem of his garment, I will be made whole." She stretches with all her might towards the Lord's feet, but she misses. "I will get to the Lord!" she says. She reaches again and this time she continues to streeeeeeetch. Suddenly, she realizes that she is no longer bleeding. The cycle has ceased! The pain is gone! She quietly observes, "Surely, this is God!" When she touched Him, He touched her.

When you touch Him, He touches you.

POWER QUESTION
Where do you need God to touch you? How is He calling you to touch Him?

POWER THOUGHT
When I touch Him, He touches me.

POWER PRAYER
Recall a time when God preformed something great in your life. Begin to thank Him. Pray:

Father, I enter into your gates with thanks and into your courts with praise. I remember [miracle or move of God]. Thank you. Thank you for touching me. Thank you for your compassion and grace. There is none like you. No one else can touch my life like you. To you be all majesty, dominion and might, forever. Bless the Lord, oh my soul. Let all that is within me bless your name. I choose to touch you today with all my heart and I look forward to your touch.

An Eternal Legacy

"Your renown endures through all generations." — Psalm 102:12

All of your friends are there. Your family members are there, as well as friends of your family. The music is soft and solemn. The conversations are minimal and pensive. The smell of fresh flowers pervades the room. Suddenly, you realize…it's your funeral.

What will be said of you? What will you leave behind? What have you sought after all of your life?

In 2002, my father went home to be with the Lord. He was a man with a sixth grade education, not known by the "movers and shakers" of the world system. Yet, he made an eternal impact upon man. Consider that this man, along with my mom, raised four children that love God. His grandkids can also be found serving the Lord. He influenced the lives of many pastors, one of whom said of him, "This man makes preachers."

My father's legacy will continue because it is connected to God's legacy.

Whatever you want your legacy to be, you must live that way right now. The degree to which you and I live our lives yielded to God, will determine our impact on the world. God's legacy endures forever. Get connected to Him, and your legacy will endure also.

POWER QUESTION
What impact are you having in your world? What is your legacy? What do you want your legacy to be?

POWER THOUGHT
I live out a legacy of honoring God, today.

POWER PRAYER
Father thank you, for the legacy of Jesus Christ that is alive and well in millions of lives today. Thank you that Jesus showed us the way. Help me to be so connected and in tune with you that the legacy of Jesus might be made real in and through me today. I choose you again and again. And because of you working in me to do of your good pleasure, I am living a lasting legacy for your glory. Let your legacy live on through me.

Doing His Will

"I delight to do thy will, O my God." — Psalm 40:8

Isn't it amazing how pleasing God is so fulfilling? Equally amazing is how we forget the joy of pleasing God when He is not the object of our devotion. That is, when we fall away from seeking God, other things seem to be more fun and fulfilling than God. But that fun is often short-lived and not true.

When God is not our focus we slowly move away from Him by not taking heed to the small things. Just like the slow death of a crab in heating water, we end up lifeless. And we forget that life is found in pleasing God! Life is found in taking heed to the small things.

You've heard that "the devil is in the details." The truth is that God is in the details and the devil doesn't want you to pay any attention to them. Look at the details God gave Moses for the tabernacle. Or, the details He gave Noah for the ark. Or, the details Jesus gave the seventy when He sent them out. Or, the detail God gave to Joshua, "March around the wall seven times." Knowing and implementing the details is where God is manifested.

Move closer to God today and get His vision. Get His input on your plans and work. Be actively dependent upon God. Take heed to the things today that don't appear important. A blessing is there for you. Maybe a blessing is there for your neighbor.

POWER QUESTION
What is God's will for you in this season of your life? What do you need to do to remove any hindrances?

POWER THOUGHT

I am actively dependent upon God. I take heed to the things today that don't appear important. A blessing is there for me.

POWER PRAYER

There are lots of things competing for my attention, Lord. But, today I choose to prioritize you and your will. Through your grace, help me to focus on the details of your will so that I may please you. In all things, Father, nevertheless not my will but yours be done.

Rest

"...and He rested." — Genesis 2:2

How often do you rest? The Scriptures say God rested, shouldn't you?

The concept of Sabbath is good, regardless of your doctrine. Everyone is moving fast, running to and fro, working on his or her life program, and looking forward to some immediate day of rest. The hard reality is that for most people, that day never comes. Jesus tells us, "Be anxious for nothing." Nothing! "Let your request be made known unto God."

Yes, we must work. Equally true is the fact that we must also rest. Rest is a refresher. Rest is spiritual. Rest allows us to shut down the things that distract us, and re-group. Because of rest, we can see God and hear His word more clearly.

Be committed to taking time off physically, emotionally, and mentally. It is the will of God. Be more like God, work *and* rest.

POWER QUESTION
What is more important work or rest? Why did God rest?

POWER THOUGHT
Since God rested, so do I.
I am like God: I work AND rest

POWER PRAYER
Father, in this fast-paced world teach me to rest. I will wait upon you Almighty God in a place of rest, and you will be glorified.

Yield It

"And he cast it upon the ground, and it became a serpent."
Exodus 4:3

Moses did not realize that his rod, not submitted to God, was a serpent. When he cast the rod down and it became a serpent, he was surprised. But should he have been? Things in our lives (gifts, talents, money, relationships, etc.) remain evil instruments if they are not yielded to God.

Isn't it interesting that the things in life that can bring us success and happiness are the same things that can bring us pain and shame?

When I was a kid my father told me, "Son there are three things that can destroy a man...money, women, and power." Throughout life I have seen men destroyed because of the abuse of those very things.

There is nothing inherently wrong with "money, women, or power," but when our hearts are not right toward God in those areas, we corrupt our relationships to them. The places where Jesus is not Lord are the places that will ultimately fail. There is no getting around it. So, if Jesus is not Lord of your relationships to the opposite sex, you will experience problems in that area. If Jesus is not Lord of your checkbook, your money will bring you torment, even if you have a lot of it. If Jesus is not Lord of your influence, you will end up prideful, and "pride comes before a fall."

Yield your money, relationship, influence, etc. to God, and just like Moses, your rod will become a tool of God that will benefit you, your family, and your community.

POWER QUESTION
To what extent have you given God privilege in your life? What do you think you will lose if you yield to God? What do you gain?

POWER THOUGHT
Jesus, you are Lord over all the areas of my life.

POWER PRAYER
Jesus, you are Lord of everything — Lord of my mind, Lord of my finances, Lord of my relationships. Lord of all. Your Word says that you are Lord of lords. Because of your lordship, I submit and render my all to you. I choose success today — I choose your Lordship over my life.

Only by Grace

"For by grace are ye saved through faith..." — Eph 2:8

I love my son. As a result, he lives in my grace. He doesn't have to do anything for my grace. Even when he is not a "good boy," my grace is upon him. The more he looks at me in faith, with those eyes that say, "My daddy can do anything," the more I want to extend grace towards him. He can work to do all the right things, for which I'll applaud him, but I have extended grace towards him simply because he is my son and he looks up to me.

There is a worship song that goes:

Only by grace can we enter.
Only by grace can we stand.
Not by our human endeavor,
But by the blood of the Lamb.

The grace of God has been extended to us because of the risen Lord. So, while we must "work out our soul salvation," let us remember that it is only by grace. It is more liberating to know that Jesus was, is, and always will be the reason why we can know God and live abundantly. Grace through faith keeps us focused on and connected to God.

It is very easy to depend upon your own abilities and work, instead of the grace of God. Depend less upon yourself. Let Christ live His life through you.

POWER QUESTION
To what extent do you rely upon the grace of God as your motivator versus gaining glory through your work?

POWER THOUGHT
God's grace does not need my help, only my faith.

POWER PRAYER
Lord, your grace is still amazing. Father, I thank you that Jesus completed the work for me and that I have already received your liberating grace. Help me to depend less on my ability and more upon your grace. I yield to you today, so be glorified in me. Teach me to walk in your grace and extend it to others today.

He Is Your "I Am"

"...Before Abraham was, I AM." — John 8:58

Driving along the George Washington Parkway is a treat for me. This parkway is a very scenic ten-mile stretch of road in Northern Virginia that is surrounded by trees and runs parallel to the Potomac River. It's a peaceful ride, especially when you are traveling out of the "hustle and bustle" of Washington, DC. One morning while enjoying the ride, I turned the radio off, and began to pray, "Lord, thank you for being my Father and my Friend."

Somehow, those words blessed me. Maybe the prayer was from God. I began to think about how God is everything to me – Father, Friend, Counselor, Teacher, Protector, Lord, Provider, Redeemer. The list goes on. How blessed it is to have a relationship with Him! Everything you need is found in Him.

What do you need today? For a lost world, Jesus says, "I AM." For success in that God-given business venture, Jesus says, "I AM." For your goals and dreams, Jesus says, "I AM." For all, in all, and through all, Jesus is "I AM."

Know HIM today and live! Experience Him as your "I AM." You will find yourself driving along life's best highway.

POWER QUESTION
What does it take for you to become aware of the great "I AM" in your home and business life?

POWER THOUGHT
Everything I need is found in Him. Jesus is the eternal "I AM."

POWER PRAYER
Oh, how I praise you mighty God. You are my source and my strength. You are my light and life. You alone are my peace and my passion. Who can stand against you? Who can give you counsel? Who can come before you? No one! For, "you are God all by yourself. You need no one else." You are the great I AM. You are my I AM. Thank you for keeping me and being with me along life's highway. You turn my dirt road into a beautiful parkway. I praise you, the great I AM.

Be Sober And Vigilant

"Be sober, be vigilant; because your adversary the devil...seeks whom he may devour" — 1 Peter 5:8

The word sober is defined as, marked by seriousness, gravity, or solemnity of character or conduct; self-restraint. The word vigilant is defined as, on the alert; aware.

At my place of work, there are a couple of guys with black belts in karate that spar occasionally. One of the things I like to do while watching them beat each other up, is to look at their eyes. There is a certain vigilance that each has, because each one knows that the other is looking for an opportunity, a moment when the opponent is slacking off, to exploit him. You can see it in their eyes.

What do your eyes say? Do your eyes speak of sobriety and vigilance?

In the whole of life, where there are "principalities and powers, rulers of darkness" that want to devour you, a sober, vigilant lifestyle is crucial to your success. Your adversary, the devil, not only wants to deceive you, he wants to devour you. As Jesus revealed, the devil wants to "steal, kill, and destroy."

Praise God, there is no need to fear the enemy, for we have already won. "The fight is fixed." God has a plan. Be sober and be vigilant so that you will always win and give God the glory!

POWER QUESTION
To what extent are you aware of God's plan for your life?

POWER THOUGHT
There is no need to fear, for I have already won.

POWER PRAYER
Father, open my eyes so I may see my victory in you. Help me to live with self-restraint and alertness. Not only do I want to live life in total victory, but I also want to help others obtain the victory. I depend upon you today, Father. You are my Victor. Thanks be to God who causes me to triumph in Jesus Christ. Hallelujah!

This Day's Bread

"Give us this day our daily bread." — Matthew 6:11

Give us this day. Not tomorrow. Not yesterday…this day. This is the day that the Lord has made.

We can't change yesterday, and tomorrow is vaguely predictable. Today is our chance. Today we can experience God. Today we can serve others. Today we can live "abundantly."

The Lord's Prayer is instructive. Jesus revealed that we should ask God to give us this day. Unless the Lord gives it (whatever it is), is it worth it? The implication is that we need God's gift, His grace, and we need to ask for it. Although the prayer specifically mentions food, isn't it true that whatever we receive is better when it comes directly from God based upon His perfect will?

God wants you to live in the present reality of His blessing. He, Himself, is your daily bread.

POWER QUESTION
What does it take for you to live in the reality of God's blessing today?

POWER THOUGHT
God, Himself, is my daily bread.

POWER PRAYER
Father, give me this day. For this day only has meaning in light of your purpose. This day cannot be fully realized without you. Father, I invite you into the affairs of my life. Amen.

Complete Redemption

"Because the creation itself also shall be delivered from the bondage of corruption..." — Romans 8:21

God is not only redeeming mankind, but ultimately, all of creation will be redeemed. This is a Christian distinctive.

The works of the devil are manifest in any activity, situation, culture, government, person, place, or thing that is not continually in proper relationship to God. When the Bible reveals that Christ has come to destroy the works of the devil, rest assured that the redemption of man, although important to God, is only the beginning of what God is doing. God is establishing a Kingdom that begins with the divine rule of God in the hearts of mankind and extends to everything else that is created. For this reason, every work of evil must be destroyed. Where there is injustice, we must confront it; where there is strife, we must resist; where there is despair, we must bring the "blessed hope."

We all have a mission and function in the Kingdom of God. Our mission is clear, "go into all the world and make disciples." Our functions may vary. However, each of us has been given a place to destroy the works of the devil and demonstrate the glory of God.

POWER QUESTION
Where have you been assigned to destroy the works of the devil?

POWER THOUGHT
Where there is injustice, I confront it; where there is strife, I resist

it; where there is despair, I bring the "blessed hope."

POWER PRAYER

Lord, your Kingdom come, your will be done in earth as it is in heaven. Yours is the Kingdom, the power, and the glory, forever. Let your will be done in me. Thank You for including me in Your plan. Amen.

Fight To Know

"That I may know Him." — Philippians 3:10

We are in spiritual war. How easy it is to forget that fact, especially when things are going well. However, it is precisely when everything is working out fine that we need to be more conscientious. "Woe to them who are at ease in Zion."

The war is not about whether or not we have successful careers or are adding more members to a church roster. The war is about knowing God and "destroying the works of the devil." The enemy wants to separate us from God. That's what the war has always been about. Read Genesis chapter 3. The cause and effect of Adam's sin was separation from God.

Remember the story Jesus told of the people who cast out devils in His name, who fed the poor, and more? You will recall that Jesus said to them, "That's all cool, but I never knew you!" The struggle is to know Him. The moment you and I cease to consciously experience God is the moment we begin to fail.

Paul had this in perspective. He understood that nothing is more important than knowing God. His quest was, "that I may know Him."

Knowing God is the fuel of the Christian life.

POWER QUESTION
Do you spend more of your time working for God or knowing God? Why?

POWER THOUGHT
When everything is working out fine, I will be more conscientious. I consciously experience God and therefore I win.

POWER PRAYER
Father, I am after one thing and one thing only: to be found in your presence. I want to know you. I want to know you more. Reveal yourself to me today as I worship you. For, in your presence there is fullness of joy. You are my desire, oh God. May I see you today in all that I see and hear. I look for you. I long for you Father. You are my desire.

Where Are You?

*"Seek ye the Lord while he may be found,
call ye upon Him while He is near" — Isaiah 55:6*

Today's Scripture implies that there is a time when God "may be found" and a time when "He is near." Thus, we can safely conclude that there are times when God will not be found and when He is not near.

Have you ever attempted to pray and wondered, "God, where are you?" Well, before you thought to ask, God had already asked the same question of you. Recall the story of Adam. After Adam chose to act independently of God (sin), God visited the Garden of Eden.

God's first question was not, "Adam, what have you done?" Instead, God asked, "Where are you?" I imagine God thinking, "Adam we were so close. We did everything together. Not only were we Creator and created, but we were friends. I provided everything you needed and things that you didn't even know you wanted. But then you left me. Where are you?"

It is not so much that God separates Himself from us; but we separate ourselves from Him. And the longer we wait to be reconciled to God, the more difficult it becomes to "find God." It is at this time that we begin to buy into other thoughts and philosophies, and find ourselves viewing God in our own image. Soon, it becomes very difficult to find God, for we are only looking at ourselves.

Stay connected to God today through prayer, worship, and active listening to Him.

POWER QUESTION
Is your view of God a reflection of your values, or is your view based on your knowledge of God gained through intimacy with Him?

POWER THOUGHT
God does not separate Himself from me.

POWER PRAYER
Father, I'm choosing right now to stay with you. I'm not going to leave this holy place. It's where I want to be – right where you are. Praise you. (Now offer God praise in your own words.)

The Uncommon

"Launch out into the deep" — Luke 5:4

The disciples were out fishing, but they were not catching any fish. They sat in the same place for several hours but they were not producing. Have you ever been there? Then Jesus stepped on the scene and gave them a Word. "You guys are in an all-too-common place. Move from your place of comfort. Go further out. Do that which is uncommon. Launch out into the deep." When they acted upon Jesus' Word and did that which was uncommon to them, they achieved their goals.

What do you want to accomplish today? God's ability in you, and his grace upon you, is most of what you need to succeed, but it is not enough. What remains is your decision to succeed by persistent work through faith. It is not enough to have faith; we must work. It is not enough to work; we must have faith.

When your work surpasses the mundane and requires more than you have, then you need "the faith of God." As God leads you, launch out into the deep. That is where you will find, not only the "God kind of faith," but the God kind of life.

Seek to advance beyond what is common...risk and excel!

POWER QUESTION
What is the most important place in your life, where you are mediocre?

POWER THOUGHT

God is able to do exceeding, abundantly above all that I ask or think, according to the power at work in me.

POWER PRAYER

Father, You are a Person of Your Word. If You say it, it is so. You said that through faith in You, I could move mountains. There are mountains in my life to be moved today. There are opportunities to serve You and increase today. Thank You for giving me the power to do the uncommon. As I take action according to Your Word, grant me your grace in Jesus' name. Amen.

Just Do It

"Whatsoever He saith unto you, do it." — John 2:5

I used to go to parties in college and would often find myself standing outside of the party area looking for that perfect girl. I would see a young lady that I wanted to dance with and wait too long to approach her. Later, I would notice some not-so-charming young man having a great time with "my girl." I learned that sometimes you just have to go for it. My friends would say, "Those who hesitate...spectate."

God gives you an idea and you know that the timing is right, but you wait. Then, you hear that someone else has done what you received from God. "Those who hesitate, spectate."

Don't get me wrong, we know the value of waiting on the Lord. However, sometimes we use the phrase "waiting on God" as an excuse because we are afraid, or we are too comfortable to change.

There is a time to wait and a time to move. When God told Abraham, "get thee out of thy country," it was not the time to wait. When Jesus told the disciples "follow me," it was not the time to wait.

When the light is red...Wait. But when the light is green...Go. Otherwise you hinder your progress and the progress of those around you. Commune with God enough to be sure of His voice. Then, whatever He says to you, do it!

POWER QUESTION
Do you include what God says to you on your daily calendar or to-do lists?

POWER THOUGHT

I use the phrase "waiting on God" only when I'm at peace with God's timing, never as an excuse because I am afraid, or I am to comfortable to change.

POWER PRAYER

Father, as you speak I will move. Until you speak, I will consider my ways. I look to you for direction and know that when I step in faith today, you will cover me. For, I am not after my own will but yours. You are my helper and my healer. You are my strength and my salvation. Speak Lord and I will obey. Speak to my heart. (Pause and consider what the Lord is saying.)

Just Obey It

"To obey is better..." – 1 Samuel 15:22

There is no one more loyal than God. As long as we obey Him, we are guaranteed that He will fight for us. There is no way we can lose. But, obedience is the leveraging point.

What has God spoken to you? Or, what do you know to do that you have not done? Your success/victory is in your obedience.

The more we obey God, the more we realize that He is sincerely more committed to us than the commandments He gives us. The less we obey, the more we think that God's Word is too constricting. However, God only wants to give us "abundant life."

Simple everyday obedience to God is where true life is found. Ask God to direct you today, and obey. Then live!

POWER QUESTION
What three things will you do today to help you obey God in the things that you have been putting off?

POWER THOUGHT
The more I obey God, the more I realize that He is sincerely more committed to me than simply the commandments He gives me.

POWER PRAYER
Speak Lord and I will obey. Speak to my heart. *(Pause and consider what the Lord is saying.)*

Most Important

"If you have faith as a grain of mustard seed..." — Matthew 17:20

The "presence of God" is not more important than God. The "anointing of God" is not more important than God. The "power of God" is not more important than God. Never be more impressed with the manifestations of God, than with God Himself.

Don't pray for more anointing. Pray for more "wisdom and revelation in the knowledge of HIM." Don't pray for more power, for it's not by power, nor by might, but by HIM.

The disciples asked Jesus for more faith. The Lord was quick to point out that "mustard seed" faith was all they needed. This is true because when we are approaching the Sovereign God, He Himself is enough.

By our prayers for more faith, power, anointing, etc., each of us must ask, "Do I really believe God?" or "Do I believe in the *things* of God?"

This is not to deny the value and need for the things of God. But nothing, not even the spiritual things we get excited about, should preoccupy us more than God Himself. Once we know Him, it does not take much faith to move mountains.

Knowing God is most important.

POWER QUESTION
Spiritually speaking, what is your preoccupation?

POWER THOUGHT

I am impressed with God Himself more than the manifestations of God.

POWER PRAYER

Who is like the Lord? Nobody! What magnificent accomplishment or activity can measure up to the splendor and glory of my God? Nothing! Father, I desire to see you simply for who you are today. Reveal yourself to me as I work, rest, and play. Show me your glory as I enter your dwelling place. You alone are worthy! Nothing I desire or have seen, compares to you.

Hot Pursuit

"The full soul loathes a honeycomb; but to the hungry soul every bitter thing is sweet." — Proverbs 27:7

Are you fully engaged in life or are you satisfied? Show me a person who is satisfied and I will show you someone loathing and reactive. Show me a person hungry and I'll show you someone focused and proactive.

Satisfaction is not contentment. I'm sure, Tiger Woods is content with his victory, but still not yet satisfied with his play. Dizzy Gillespie was content with a lot of his music, but he was not satisfied with his mastery of his horn. There are other challenges to overcome.

Maybe, that's why change is a constant in life. Maybe, that's why life is composed of hills and valleys. Otherwise, we might not push.

Are you hungry for God?

The religious answer is always, yes. However, the proof is whether you and I are seeking after God "like the deer pants for water."

Never be satisfied with a limited knowledge of God. No matter how many times you've heard the gospel, the Bible is full of "progressive revelation."

Pursue!

POWER QUESTION
What do you need to receive from the Father in order to act more

deliberately toward knowing Him?

POWER THOUGHT
I am not satisfied with a limited knowledge of God. No matter how many times I have heard the gospel, the Bible is full of "progressive revelation."

POWER PRAYER
Father, I am content, but not satisfied. I am grateful for what you have done for, in, and through me. But, I am not satisfied. I want more of you. Help me to see more of you. Reveal yourself to me as I study your word, which is a light for my path. I am hungry for you. You are the best in me! Show me your glory, so that I may give you more glory. You are glorious. Help me to show forth your glory to the nations. Oh that we may see your glory manifested in the earth.

Spiritual Solutions

*"For the flesh lusts against the Spirit,
and the Spirit against the flesh"* — Galatians 5:17

The flesh is not simply lust, covetousness, greed, gluttony, etc. Ultimately, the flesh is the human will's resistance to God.

Many of us have heard sermons on how important it is to "crucify the flesh," because the flesh is contrary to the Spirit. And that's good. However, there is more. The Spirit is contrary to the flesh and the implications of this are important for our lives. Instead of focusing on the flesh, we need to focus on what the Spirit is doing.

Because the Spirit wars against the flesh, when we approach God for a solution, there will be something in His solution, which will confront the flesh. This is where many people decide that God is not for them. You cannot have God's solution and no contention with the flesh. Whenever God speaks, your will must surrender. If it doesn't, you can kiss the "true solution" goodbye.

Sure, there are counterfeit solutions that work temporarily. But, we miss abundant life and solutions that have eternal impact when we fail to surrender as the Spirit wars against the flesh.

The same man that said, "Nevertheless, not my will, but thine be done," is He of whom God said, "Every knee shall bow." When we surrender our wills to God, God exalts us for His glory.

As you pray for solutions, also pray for a revelation of the thing(s) that must *change in you* in order for the solution to be realized.

POWER QUESTION
Do you include what God says to you on your calendar or to-do lists?

POWER THOUGHT
As I pray for solutions, I also pray for a revelation of the thing(s) that must change in me in order for the solution to be realized.

POWER PRAYER:
Lord, I no longer want counterfeit solutions. I want real solutions that begin and end with You. Show me where Your Spirit is warring against my flesh and grant me the victory, in Jesus' name, amen.

The Art Of Spiritual War

"...The gates of Hell shall not prevail against it." – Matthew 16:18

The gates of Hell shall not prevail against us! Gates are for defense. The evil one wants to keep us out of his territory because he knows he cannot win. Unfortunately, some of us are not sure we can win either. "There are giants in the land," we say.

How strong are you in the Lord? Your strength can be measured by the extent to which you are offensive towards the Kingdom of darkness.

Examine your prayers. If a majority of your prayers are for you and yours that is an indicator that you still have not reached God. Certainly, we need to pray for ourselves, but at some point our focus needs to turn to those who are without –without God, without family, without health, without food, just without! The Christian life is not simply about overcoming sin and the evil one. This way of life is about experiencing God in such a way that we penetrate the gates of hell. Unfortunately, many of us live in isolation from the world and we never get to the "gates" or penetrate them.

However, as you experience God you will begin to act like Him, penetrating Hell's gates and establishing the Kingdom. The real issue, the bottom-line, the thing that matters most is "Are you experiencing God?"

POWER QUESTION
Where are the gates of Hell in your sphere of influence? What must you do, with God, to prevail?

POWER THOUGHT
The Christian life is about experiencing God in such a way that I penetrate the gates of Hell.

POWER PRAYER
Father, lead me to that person on my job or in my community that is looking for You. Give me the wisdom and courage to approach them like Jesus and have a ready Word that will move them closer to You.

Remember God

"They remembered not his hand..." — Psalm 78:42

It is amazing how easy it is to forget the power of God. There have been times when I have looked up and realized, "Wow! I'm really not trusting God here."

Has that ever happened to you? Going along with your daily activities and proceeding as if God was not there. Then some sort of crisis hits, big or small, and you begin to think about God. Only to realize that if your focus had been on God in the first place, the crisis may not have come, or you would have been better prepared for it. Been there, done that?

When we think about who God is, and recall "his works of old" in our lives, worship results! We begin to remember, "Nothing is impossible with God." Questions like, "Is anything too hard for God?" begin to surface in our hearts. Then our vision changes and we "have the confidence that if we ask anything according to His will, He hears us." The world, the challenges, and the evil seem so small in the light of God's presence.

Let us not be like Israel, as seen in Psalm 78, who failed to remember the power of God. Let us spend time communing with God, which is the ultimate goal of prayer, so that we see Him. When we see Him, we shall be like Him, and then nothing is impossible to those who believe.

Remember the hand of God.

POWER QUESTION
What has God done for you lately?

POWER THOUGHT
When I think about who God is, and recall "his works of old" in my life, worship results.

POWER PRAYER
Father, thank you! (Begin to thank God for all that he means to you and has done for you.)

Purposeful Love

"For God so loved the world that He gave His only begotten Son that whosoever believes on Him should not perish but have everlasting life." — John 3:16

Love must have a purpose. God's love was not some mystic attitude towards us. It was an activity of God's heart that sought to meet our true need – salvation. His love has purpose.

When you love your spouse, family members, friends, co-workers, or neighbors, what is your purpose? Look for true needs in the lives of your spouse, family members, friends, co-workers, and neighbors and set your love toward those needs. The degree to which you seek to serve people, purposing (or intent) to meet their needs, is a measure of your love.

Be like God, set your heart on the needs of those you love. Give with your whole heart seeking their benefit. Do it "on purpose," for purpose is the distinguishing factor in love. That is, purpose makes our love effective.

POWER QUESTION
To what degree are you focused on the needs of those you love?

POWER THOUGHT
The degree to which I seek to serve peoples true needs is a measure of my love.

POWER PRAYER

Father, show me the emotional or spiritual need in [name of loved one]'s life. I pray oh God, that you will heal them in that area. [Spend some time praying for that person.] Teach me how to love like you love. Teach me to give of myself, to lose my life for the sake of others, for your Kingdom.

Balance Is Key

*"I make a decree, that in every dominion of my kingdom
men tremble and fear before the God of Daniel:
for He is the living God." — Daniel 6:26*

Daniel is a favorite of mine for two reasons. First, he understood his utter dependence upon God. Second, he had an excellent spirit.

Often people have either one trait or the other. There is the person who is totally "sold out" to God but their commitment to excellence leaves something to be desired. Then, there are others who endeavor to achieve excellence even if it means sacrificing a meaningful relationship with God. However, it is possible to live in excellence and have a strong relationship with God. Daniel's life reveals that a person can truly know God and maintain excellence - in that order.

Daniel stood before kings, yet, that was not where his worth was found. In the midst of tremendous crisis, he did not compromise his beliefs for the sake of his position. In the end, the king, Darius, was convinced that Daniel's God was God.

As God's people maintain this unique balance of commitment to God and excellence, our lives will preach. Then, doors will open for us with opportunities to save our communities. And people will know that our God is God. Balance is the key.

POWER QUESTION
To what extent are the people in your life convinced that God is God

because of your clear commitment to Him and your excellence?

POWER THOUGHT
I live in excellence, while maintaining a strong relationship with God.

POWER PRAYER
Oh Lord, how excellent is your name. Since you are excellent, I am excellent, because you are in me. The seed of excellence is in me. Let it come forth, oh Lord, as I yield to you. Let me not try to act excellently of mine own accord. Let me simply be who you call me to be: a person of excellent spirit. Use that excellence for your glory, Father, and draw men to you, as a result. Oh Lord, how excellent is your name in all the earth. How excellent is your name in me.

Wise Witness

"He that wins souls is wise." – Proverbs 11:30

Every logical argument starts with a premise and that premise drives the argument. A conclusion must be traced directly back to the premise(s) in order for an argument to be logical.

Many times, Christians have trouble with the conclusions of non-Christians because their conclusions are not the same as ours. We argue against their conclusions with statements like, "Abortion is wrong," "Homosexuality is of the devil," etc. The arguments get more fervent and frequent but we rarely find an increase in the percentage of people being won to Jesus as a result. Is it because we argue the wrong thing? Is it because we should take a closer look at the premises of the world that drives their conclusions?

For example, one of the premises of the abortion rights advocates is that "a woman has the right to do with her body as she wills." We need to take a closer look at that premise, as opposed to simply telling them, "You are wrong." You see, the correct premise is that a woman's body does not belong to her but to God.

The goal of the Christian life is not to "prove" what we believe is right, but to point people to the truth – Jesus. Unless people see Jesus for who He is, all of our arguments are simply other logical approaches to a problem. This is accomplished through communion with God that finds its way into practical, measurable results in your life.

POWER QUESTION
Is God proven through your life?

POWER THOUGHT
My goal is not to "prove" what I believe is right, but to point people to Jesus.

POWER PRAYER
Father, as I yield to you in secret prayer show me the person that you want me to reach today. I thank you for the wisdom to compel that person to commit to Jesus. When you lead, I will follow. All the glory is yours for the great things you will do in that person's life.

What Did You Say?

*"A soft answer turns away wrath,
but grievous words stir up anger." – Proverbs 15:1*

I do not like to be closely followed while driving. In fact, one morning someone was tailing me, maybe because 60 mph in a 55 mph zone is simply too slow. I must say, there was a temptation for me to call the guy a "FOOL." But I "held my peace," and in the privacy of my car, softly called the infamous trailer a "CLOWN" instead. I know that is not good either, but its better. Right?

The story could have gone a different way. The headline could have been, "Bruce Clark, an alleged devout Christian, was arrested today for stopping traffic on the George Washington Parkway, after being tailed by a man infamously known as 'FOOL'. The altercation ended with Mr. Fool having a broken arm and a rather large dent on the hood of his car from repeated strikes with a baseball bat."

We may not have the ability to control other's actions, but we do have the ability to control our reaction.

Today when that "trying situation" comes, remember the scripture above and take control of the situation by carefully choosing and speaking the right words.

Words change things.

POWER QUESTION
To what extent is your reality also a reflection of your words?

POWER THOUGHT

I am not controlled by circumstances. Rather, I take control of every situation by carefully choosing and speaking the right words.

POWER PRAYER

Lord, your Word have I hid in my heart that I may not sin against you. Teach me to observe your words today. May my words be consistent with your words; for your Word will never fail. I will speak those things that bring life. Thank you for the integrity of your Word. (Begin to praise God for His Word.)

Reconciliation – God's Agenda

"God was in Christ reconciling the world...and hath committed unto us the word of reconciliation." — II Corinthians 5:19

I was at a dinner one night with some very prestigious people of different races. One of them was the chairperson of a major Christian organization, and we asked him some hard questions about how serious his colleagues were taking the issue of racial reconciliation. To my pleasure, his bottom line was that God was committed to it and because of that, regardless of where others are at this time, reconciliation will happen because it is God's plan. Amen.

What God is doing is very clear. He is bringing people to Himself, and then bringing people together - in that order. Only God can connect people in a way that transcends the million and one reasons why we disconnect.

Are we bringing people to God, and bringing people together? Are we bringing ourselves to God, and connecting with other people outside of our economic level, culture, race, and beliefs?

Reconciliation must be deliberate and it can only happen as a result of continual communion with God. Yet, like in every other thing, we find ourselves trying to accomplish reconciliation through programs, services, meetings, etc.

Strategy is secondary to vision, and vision that comes from God is found in fellowship with Him. So, when reconciliation burns in our hearts as a result of communion with God, our meetings will be effective. Until then, we're marking time. But, I guess marking time is better than turning back the clock.

Let's move forward toward reconciliation. God give us your mind and your heart!

POWER QUESTION
To what extent should one go out of his way to be reconciled to his neighbor?

POWER THOUGHT
Reconciliation must be deliberate and it can only happen as a result of continual communion with God.

POWER PRAYER
God give me your mind and your heart towards those that are different from me! (Stretch yourself here. Begin to pray for the areas in your life where you resist reconciliation. Cry out to God for change.)

The Path To Freedom

"Stand fast in the liberty wherewith Christ has made you free, and be not entangled again with the yoke of bondage." — *Galatians 5:1*

God has called us to a life that draws from Him, not a life that focuses simply on deeds. Christians often use the phrase "a Spirit-controlled life." But is that a realistic concept? Does God want to control us? I don't think so, because if he did is that freedom?

The great jazz drummer, Elvin Jones said, "There can be no freedom without control." But, it is not God that controls us. We are controlled by our decisions. And our decisions flow out of our will.

The Christian life is about abandonment. It is the abandonment of our will to His. In so doing, as an act of our will, we endeavor to please God. The Christian life is not a program we start, or a list of do's and dont's that we follow. It is not religion or tradition. It is freedom.

It is the freedom Jesus had when He changed water to wine at a party, and when He healed on the Sabbath. It is not regulated. It is natural. The Christian life is one where we yield ourselves to God in every situation. We obey him even at the risk of looking silly. This is true freedom.

You are free in Christ. And that freedom will manifest as you abandon your will to God's will.

POWER QUESTION
To what degree are you free?

POWER THOUGHT
My freedom manifests as I abandon my will to God's will.

POWER PRAYER
Lord Jesus, as I continue in your Word, I will know the truth, and the truth will make me free. You are Truth. Your Words are truth. Let your truth bring freedom to the surface of my life. In all things, I praise you. You have set me free. Where your Spirit is, there is freedom. I am free, because your Spirit is in me. Draw me closer, Spirit of Freedom. May others see the freedom you have given me, and say, "What must I do to be like you?" May they see you, Lord. I am free to declare your truth to them. And they will be free too. Thank you Jesus.

Oh Glory

"All have sinned and fallen short of the glory of God."
— Rom 3:23

The crisis of sin, which is being, acting, or thinking independent of God, has been resolved through Christ. But the crisis of being less than what we are created to be is only resolved through our persistent effort to live our lives totally dependent on God, focused, excellent, and determined.

The life God intends for us is not about sin, it is about glory. As Peter told us, "God has called us to *glory* and *virtue*."

However, we fall short of that glory, not only through sin, but through vices like mediocrity, conformity, and distractions. The Word tells us to *add* to our faith – virtue, knowledge, temperance, patience, godliness, brotherly kindness and love. What are you adding to your faith?

Is our message to the world, of condemnation of sin, simply a statement of self-righteousness? Jesus didn't talk a lot about the problem. He offered a solution – Himself. Many times we focus on sin because of our failure to excel. Can we say to the world like Peter did, "Look on us?" For some of us, it may not be that we have sinful lifestyles, but that we have "fallen short of the glory of God."

Press on to glory. Strive for the mastery of your work and of your relationship with God. Excel! And return to God the glory that you will receive.

POWER QUESTION
What are you adding to your faith?

POWER THOUGHT
God has called me to glory and virtue.

POWER PRAYER
Lord, show me where I am mediocre and give me the courage to face it. Father, lead me to excellence and be glorified! You have not made me to just get by. You have made me in your image. You have made me glorious and virtuous. Let your character be manifested in me.

Anointed For What?

"The Spirit of the Lord is upon me because He hath anointed me to preach the gospel to the poor..."—Luke 4:18

Isn't it amazing how we ask God to anoint us for everything except giving the good news to those who are without God? "Lord, anoint my marriage. Lord, anoint me on my job." While there is nothing wrong with asking God to approve and give favor to the things that concern you, the anointing is for ministry.

Jesus, our eternal example, made it clear in his inaugural address. "God has anointed me to serve people." The result of Jesus' anointing was changed lives. The result was not simply self-gratification, but meeting the true needs of people.

Except for God and His glory, there is nothing more important than people; not our doctrine, nor our liturgy; and not our excellence, nor our vision. The Spirit of the Lord has anointed us to meet needs here on earth.

The anointing is for ministry.

POWER QUESTION
Who are you anointed to serve?

POWER THOUGHT
I am anointed for ministry, right where I am.

POWER PRAYER
Father, I thank you for baptizing me in your Spirit, anointing me to

serve others on your behalf. Show me who to serve today. As I walk with you, lead me to those that you want to reach. Heal and deliver, oh Lord. Use me for your glory. I am an ambassador for Christ, anointed and appointed for the glory of God. Praise your name, oh Lord.

Monday's Opportunity

"For a just man falls seven times and rises up again..."
—Proverbs 24:16

When my son was nine-months old, he started to crawl and was all over the place. But he was not satisfied with crawling. Upon the slightest opportunity, he would grab a chair or a wall and pull himself up to stand. And then he would fall. Sometimes he would land pretty hard and his head might hit the floor. But behold, he would get up yet another time to do it all over again. Soon after, he learned to walk because he kept getting up and starting over again.

What did you want to accomplish last week, but didn't? How many times have you failed at _____ ? *(Fill in the blank.)*

It's going to be ok! Just keep getting up.

Monday morning presents another opportunity to succeed. Thank God it's Monday, because you and I can start all over again.

And with the grace of God at work in your life, how can you lose as you continue to persist? You will win, because when you get back up, God is right there to strengthen you.

POWER QUESTION
What will it take for you to continue going after God?

POWER THOUGHT
Today I have another new opportunity to succeed.

POWER PRAYER

Lord, thank you for your mercy. It is new every morning. Father, I trust you. You have given me the strength to get up and start again. To you are all the glory, honor, and dominion.

Clear Signs

"An evil and adulterous generation seeks a sign."
— Matthew 12:39

"If only God would give me some clear sign! Like making a large deposit in my name at a Swiss bank." – A Hollywood Producer

If Mr. Hollywood only knew, God gives us signs all the time. Unfortunately, we don't always want to see those signs or they are not the signs we want. We want the signs to be consistent with our values or desires. But God's "thoughts are not our thoughts and [His] ways not our ways."

Not that there is anything wrong with a large deposit at a Swiss bank. God is not against that. The question is, "What purpose would it serve?" If God were to deposit money in a bank for you, would you then give Him the freedom to tell you what to do with it?

That sign may not be a good one for you.

But the signs that God does exist and wants to be in relationship with you are here. God is speaking to you through "a still small voice," a friend or family member, a pastor, or a circumstance. What is He saying?

To clearly understand what God is saying, assess what you really want (like a large Swiss Bank account). What you want may be the thing that hinders your perception of what God is saying. Pray for clarity.

God is speaking to you. And whatever it is, it's for your good. It is good!

POWER QUESTION
Through what means has God spoken to you within the last thirty days?

POWER THOUGHT
God is speaking to me through "a still small voice," a friend or family member, a pastor, or a circumstance.

POWER PRAYER:
Father, thank you for speaking to me. I am your sheep and I hear your voice. Help me to be open to the various ways you speak to me. Open my ears, Lord, and help me to listen. Give me revelation as I study your Word. Oh, that I may see you and know you. Your voice is pleasant and powerful. Your Word is comforting and provoking. You are the source of all wisdom and knowledge. May I not seek a sign, but only you.

Go Sow, Go Reap

"...He that sows to the Spirit shall reap life everlasting."
— Galatians 6:8

Abundant life isn't an existence where we have everything we want, when we want it, and for how long we want it. On this earth that's impossible because of the nature of sin that exists in our hearts. Evil abounds and it affects all of us in some form or fashion.

But we can be "delivered from evil." We can choose every day, at the moment of each decision, to "sow to the Spirit." That is, we can do the things that please God. Every time we do what is pleasing to God, we are sowing spiritual seed. The fruit of this seed is life everlasting that we experience right here on earth.

Whatever you sow you will reap.

Plant seeds of kindness; seeds of faith; seeds of love; seeds of patience; seeds of encouragement to someone who needs it; seeds of finances to someone who is without; seeds of prayer; seeds of support to your leaders; seeds of hope and Godly-vision to your followers.

Reap life, and that more abundantly!

POWER QUESTION
What seeds are you planting?

POWER THOUGHT
Everyday, I have an opportunity to live life abundantly, in the presence of God.

POWER PRAYER

Father, help me to watch over my investment of time and money. Evaluate my thoughts and words so that they align with your will. By your grace I will sow spiritual seed today, so that I might reap a harvest of Christ-like character.

How Much Do You Weigh

"Let me be weighed in the balance, that God may know my integrity." — Job 31:6

If God were to weigh your character, how would you measure? Would it be said of you, as in the words of the late Rev. F. H. Dunn, "You have been weighed in the balance, and have been found light as a feather?" Or would the Lord say, "Behold, a person of no guile?"

Most of us live in the middle. However, integrity is not neutral. Integrity is extreme.

Integrity, at its core, is doing what you know is right, regardless of the consequences. Not what is right for you, but what is right. Of course, this is where the challenge is. What exactly is *right*? The only way to know what is right is to get the wisdom of God. "If any man lacks wisdom, let him ask of God who gives liberally and upbraids not."

The balance God uses measures what we know versus what we do. The more balanced that scale, the greater degree of our integrity.

POWER QUESTION
If God were to weigh your character, how would you measure?

POWER THOUGHT
The only way to know what is right is to get the wisdom of God.

POWER PRAYER

Father, search me and know. Find the places in me where I'm not walking in integrity. Help me to be like you. There is no difference in what you say, think, and do. You are the source of true integrity. For you are your Word, and your Word is Truth. You are the truth. Oh that I might be like you. Grant unto your servant wisdom, that I might know how to live right, talk right, and be right. It's all for your glory, oh God.

Choose Patience

"But let patience have her perfect work, that you may be perfect and entire, wanting nothing." — James 1:4

One day my car battery went to that great battery retirement home in the sky. But getting it out of my car was a challenge. The post terminals were very old and I didn't have the tools to remove them properly. To compound the problem, the battery was also secured to the car's frame by a piece of rusty metal that would not budge. It was frustrating and I became impatient.

Forty minutes later, I finally wedged the battery out of the car. But wait, it is only 7:15am, and the car parts store doesn't open until 8:00am. I've got other errands to run before going to work. James 1:4 was the furthest thing from my mind.

There will always be challenges, but in each challenge we can allow the character of Christ to be revealed in and through us. *"Let patience..."* implies that it must be an act of our will. Patience is waiting to help mature us and give us what we need, but we must let it.

Choose patience over anxiety.

Someone has jokingly said, "Lord, give me patience...and I want it RIGHT NOW." It doesn't quite work that way. Patience is a continual process of acting upon the character of Jesus. This character is revealed in us through our communion with Him, causing us to be "perfect and entire, wanting nothing."

What do you want? Patience is your key.

POWER QUESTION
In your lifetime, how many times has rushing been worth it?

POWER THOUGHT
In each challenge, I allow the character of Christ to be revealed in and through me.

POWER PRAYER
Lord, thank you for giving me all the patience I need this day, in Christ. By faith and through dependence upon you, I am prepared for every challenge today.

Too Busy

"Be still and know that I am God." – Psalm 46:10

F. Scott Fitzgerald said, "There are only the pursued, the pursuing, the busy, and the tired." Which are you? Woe to the person who is not pursuing, for your enemy is waiting.

There is an old hymn which says, "Satan is on my track and he's trying to turn me back." These are not the words of one who is pursuing but one being pursued. Yet, it is clear from the scripture that we are to put the devil out of business and not vice versa. Isn't it true that "no weapon formed against [us] shall prosper?" Isn't it true that the "gates of hell shall not prevail against us?" So why is Satan on your track? Why aren't you on his?

We need to be aware of the devices of our enemy. And Satan needs to know that there is a God in Zion, and that God is in the midst of His people, so "don't even try it." Often we get too busy with church responsibilities and become tired. This is not noble, but a strategy of our enemy.

Satan says, "Ok, they are not going to come back to me so I'll get them really busy in church and doing a lot of stuff. They'll think they are ok because of the volume of their Christian activity, but they'll get so tired that they won't have the energy to fellowship with God. That will decrease their power. And we can stay in business."

Are you too busy? Are you spiritually tired? Those are indicators that you are not pursuing. Step back. Be still. Get focused. Focus your efforts on God's will and people who are in need. Pursue God. Pursue the Kingdom.

But first, be still and know that He is God.

POWER QUESTION
What is pursuing you? What are you pursuing?

POWER THOUGHT
I focus my efforts on God's will.

POWER PRAYER
I will wait on you, Almighty God. When I get tired, I'll get more focused. When I am not pursuing you, show me where I have missed it. I run to you, oh God, for you are what I am after. Give me strength to pursue you, like the deer pants for the water. My desire is to please you, to pursue you, to follow you with my whole heart.

Good Crisis

"It is good for me that I have been afflicted; that I might learn thy statues." – Psalm 119:71

Affliction is not an end for the Christian, but it is often the beginning – the beginning of a work of God in your heart.

What are you going through? It will be ok as long as you go through and not stay there, especially, emotionally. The fact that you are going through means that there is an end to the challenge. *This too, will pass.*

In the midst of every crisis, God has a plan. Seek Him. Discover what He is doing and that will strengthen you through the hard times. You will find God in the process of going through. Commit to the process, because it is there that we learn to know God. And isn't that what life is about?

The best days of your life are ahead!

POWER QUESTION
What is God saying to you in the crisis?

POWER THOUGHT
In the midst of every crisis, God has a plan.

POWER PRAYER
Father, you did not say walking with you would be comfortable. Thank you for the discomfort that leads me to you. I know that you have not changed. You delivered Joseph, you'll deliver me. You

delivered Daniel, you'll deliver me. You delivered Paul and Silas, you'll deliver me. So, I wait Father, with great expectation. My expectation is from you alone. In the midst of it all, be glorified, Lord!

One Thing Is Sure

"I am the Lord; I change not." — Malachi 3:6

Imagine me going home to my wife today and saying, "Honey, I am your husband. I change not." The implications of that statement include; I am always right; my intentions are always pure; I don't need to change.

You can imagine peace in my home flying right out of the window. The reality is that there are things in my life that I do need to change and no one knows that better than the Mrs.

Unlike me, God is always right and always pure. His integrity is always intact. He does not need to change. In this simple reality, we find the answer to many of the questions that arise when we don't understand why God allows bad things to happen, or why God says something we don't agree with. God is always right. God is always pure.

If we know that God is right and pure, then why do we leave Him for self-gratification? Why is there an internal competition between what God says is right and our personal beliefs? Why is there a lingering thought in the minds of some Christians that God and "real" fun are incompatible?

Well, the more integrity one has, the more one will believe in God's integrity. "To the pure all things are pure."

God changes not, because He is Truth, Pure, Virtuous, and the list goes on. God is solid. The more we become like Him, the more solid we become.

POWER QUESTION
What do you need to change in order to get to God?

POWER THOUGHT
The more integrity I have, the more I believe in God's integrity.

POWER PRAYER
There is one thing that is true, oh God; you will not change. Your word and your integrity are in tact. What you say you will do, you will do. Great is your faithfulness, oh Lord, my God. I will trust in you with my whole heart. Father, as you are changing me to become more like you, reveal the places and things in my life that need to change. Grant unto me the grace to take you at your word and accept that I am complete in Christ. Help me to walk in the total redemption that is in me, in Christ.

Are You Enjoying Life?

"...God, who gives us richly all things to enjoy."— I Timothy 6:17

Sometimes in life we lose things that we once held dear or enjoyed, and we don't realize how much we missed them until we get them back.

For example, I know someone who in his first semester of college spent a lot of time playing billiards. He really enjoyed the game and during that first semester, probably played pool as much as he studied. Somewhere along the way – probably after realizing that he could not get a degree or job in "pool playing" and probably after getting too many C's – he realized that his priorities needed to change. Eventually, he stopped playing. But he still loved the game.

Over the last year, his friends began playing the game and he joined them. Somewhat nostalgic with disillusions of past greatness, he found himself beginning to get good at the game again. If he would play more than three times a month, he could probably become better than he was in college.

What have you lost over the years that you really enjoyed? (Of course, you know I do not mean sins.) Have you allowed the responsibility of family, church, work, and community to hinder your enjoyment of even the simple things of life?

We must develop a view of the world that says, God wants us to enjoy life! A view that says, "If I'm not enjoying life, somewhere I am missing God." Some would say that's not very religious, but ponder its truth. The Bible reveals that one of the core values of the Kingdom of God is JOY! Unfortunately, we have "super-spiritualized" the concept of joy and neglected its impact on our work and play.

Begin to ask God to help you regain some of the fun things you may have lost to life's challenges. It's ok. God is interested in that part of your life too.

POWER QUESTION
To what extent is God committed to your enjoyment of life?

POWER THOUGHT
I maintain a view of the world that says, God wants me to enjoy life!

POWER PRAYER
Father, you give me all things to enjoy. May your joy consume me. The joy of the Lord is my strength. May my personal happiness and fun never replace or imitate the joy that is found in your presence. I choose the real thing, Father; not the counterfeit. I choose the joy of the Lord. As I am found in your presence, I receive your joy. For in your presence, Lord, there is fullness of joy and at your right hand there are eternal pleasures.

What Is Your Motivation?

"...Bless me indeed...enlarge my border... be with me ...keep me from evil." —1 Chronicles 4:10

Do you desire the blessing of God or do you think it is carnal to ask for it?

The enemy has sold the church a bill of evil that says, "Just desire enough to survive. Anything extra might lead to pride and lust." Many of God's people walk around living from day to day without vision or expectation.

The latter part of the verse above reveals that God is not averse to granting blessing and enlargement. Most people are willing to accept that. But some renounce the notion of *desiring* blessing and enlargement. Some see desiring God and desiring God's blessing as mutually exclusive.

The notions of blessings and enlargement only present problems when our hearts are not deeply rooted in the Kingdom. Is the fear and aversion of abundance a measure of one's knowledge of his lack of commitment to Jesus? Because one knows that his heart is not where it should be toward God, does he fear that blessings might steer him away from God? If so, abundance is not the problem, is it?

Jabez was wise for praying that God would be with him and keep him in the midst of God's blessing and enlargement. He was equally wise to ask God to bless him and enlarge his border.

The challenge is to not confuse the blessing of God with the world's images. The life of Jabez reveals that it is possible to be

pure in heart and desire God's blessing.
It's a matter of motive.

POWER QUESTION
What motivates you?

POWER THOUGHT
The notions of blessings and enlargement only present problems when my heart is not deeply rooted in the Kingdom.

POWER PRAYER
Father, bless me that I may be a blessing. Keep me from anything or anyone that would distract me from your purposes. Try my motives, oh God. Reveal to me my secret thoughts and ambitions, and align them with your Word. As you bless me Father, I will bless others. Most importantly, I will bless you at all times. Your praise will continually be in my mouth.

Simplicity

"the simplicity that is in Christ" – *II Corinthians 11:3*

The message of Christ and the life He has called us to is not difficult to understand. Even a child can grasp the meaning of Jesus' life. You know the story. God made man. Man separated himself from God. God reached out to man through Jesus. Man can be reconnected with God through Jesus. Life is about communion with God through Jesus and serving mankind.

Unfortunately, we cloud "the simplicity that is in Christ" with a lot of other stuff. One way that we add complexity to the Christian walk is by thinking that our empty attempts at holiness qualifies us for Christ's love. Why do we make things more complex than they really are? Many times our attempt to make this Christian walk more complex is a direct result of our failure to live out the simple truths of Christ.

However, we must make Christ the message and not "Christ-likeness." We debate theology and doctrine, which often simply serves to hide our hypocrisy.

This walk with Christ is not complex. Yet, if in your life it is, that may be an indicator that something needs fixing. And our repairs start at communion with God. Keep your heart and mind focused on the fact that it is all about Jesus. He is the reason. Look to Him for peace in the middle of complexity.

POWER QUESTION
How complex is your daily life? If you simplified your life what

would you eliminate first?

POWER THOUGHT
I watch complexity. It's an indicator that something needs fixing. And repairs start at my communion with God.

POWER PRAYER
Lord, I trust you today to speak to me though the simple things in life. By your grace, I focus on the simple fact that Jesus is alive and living through me. He is the overcomer and causes me to triumph. I look not to complexities of life, but to Jesus the Author and Finisher of my faith. Father, if I loose focus on the simplicity that is in Christ, remind me of your Word. Be pleased and glorified through my childlike faith in you.

www.ingramcontent.com/pod-product-compliance
Ingram Content Group UK Ltd.
Pitfield, Milton Keynes, MK11 3LW, UK
UKHW041955230426
12048UKWH00008B/348